Ten Thousand Birds

Birds

*New and Selected Haiku, Senryu
and Haibun*

Anatoly Kudryavitsky

First Edition: 2020
Rs. 200/-

Cyberwit.net
HIG 45 Kaushambi Kunj, Kalindipuram
Allahabad - 211011 (U.P.) India
http://www.cyberwit.net
Tel: +(91) 9415091004 +(91) (532) 2552257
E-mail: info@cyberwit.net

Printed at Repro India Limited.

Contents

Haiku 5

    Spring 7

    Summer 15

    Autumn 27

    Winter 37

The Season of No Season (Haiku and Senryu) 45

Haibun 57

Haiku

Spring

awakening
to the echo of wind chimes,
ten thousand birds and I

hazel catkins
in the mizzling rain...
a long, long dream

home town revisited –
white butterflies
in the churchyard

Vernal equinox
full moon balancing
on the ridgepole

bursting buds
on the bird-cherry
each one a soundless bell

blue patches in the sky
wind combs dried grass
for hyacinths

stairs strewn
with cherry blossom petals
piano music

after the wedding,
white butterfly clinging
to the ivy

moonlight
through the mulberry tree...
silkworms' threads

spring tide –
the reflection of a bridge
flows under the bridge

old willow
a thousand branches holding
the spring wind

one by one filling
with sunlight,
wet plum blossoms

their branches almost touch…
glass-house cherry tree
and the one outside

now you see it, now you don't
white butterfly
at Dover cliffs

sweeping wind –
petals frozen
to icy patches

from inside
the golden crocuses
a flame of dawn

power cut
moonlight reflecting
off magnolia leaves

derelict boat
among marsh marigolds –
the night floats by

wetlands
wind sings a lullaby
to a baby frog

weeping cherry tree
in the graveyard
the first to bloom

long day
a bumblebee sucks warmth
from the weary sun

departing emigrant ship...
dandelion seeds
in the wind

the scent
of globeflowers...
earthly sojourn

evening lull
a seaside cave exhaling
butterflies

Summer

bamboo stems
their memories
of the sun

sheep unmoved
in the green grass...
a slow passing of clouds

mountain tarweed –
touching its flowers
smelling your fingers

climbing a rocky ridge
in the sun,
two winged ants

lily buds
a girl in the window
blows the long flute

Waterloo Day –
through the dusty haze,
a row of cypresses

burning sunshine
splashes of orange lichen
on the dam

simmering soup pot
a scarecrow stirs
midday heat

starry night
a black and yellow ladybird
sits still

heading towards
the twin chimneys,
a two-horned snail

quiet summer day
dried streambed
preserves the ripples

doctor's surgery –
on the man's sole
a crushed butterfly

at twilight
the silent call
of a lone fruit-stalk

telegraph wires
dawn singing a song
to the nightingale

summer afterglow
the still dance of
fuchsia flowers

heat lightning
a sunflower
kisses the sun

morning clouds
the misty sun follows
an oriole's song

cloudy day
the green of water
and the green of trees

parting walk
a plover leads us away
from her nest

faces
exposed by the moonlight...
callas blooming

calm evening
the voices of
birches and aspens

twilight...
petal from
a misty-blue flower

boundary stone
the nettles
pause

Fathers' Day –
children measure old oaks
by the length of their arms

abandoned
caravan park site –
snails

Finnish knives
at the summer market –
zigzagging sun rays

ventilator off –
the sound of dragonfly
wing beats

flowering meadows –
the scent lingers
on my soles

mosquito
in Baltic amber –
its frozen flight

insomnia
a fireworks flower
glowing red

tranquil morning
a mower's shape
slashes through the mist

it's well looked after,
the grass the prisoners make
into ropes

abandoned temple
hail stones falling
on dwarf bamboo

on the steps
of the Freedom Memorial,
a discarded snake skin

empty square in Assam –
ants labour
in elephants' footsteps

grass snake
escaping into
my thought of it

moonlight
through thorny trees –
a scarlet tanager

fireflies
dancing to the rhythm
of a lighthouse beam

abandoned farm
the cry of a curlew
crosses the evening sky

inside the empty shell, snail's dreams

Autumn

autumn wind…
I yearn for the place
from where it blows

last slices of moonshine –
silverside fish
in the mirror pool

exploring a length of breath autumn wind

aspen in the rain
each leaf dripping with
the sound of autumn

amid red and green flashes
the moon enters
a tidal harbour

autumn dusk
a cat rubs its shadow
against fishermen's legs

raindrops pattering
on banana leaves
September lamplight

grey autumn day
the bright green of
angel hair algae

draughty phone-box
a little moonlight
trickling in

overgrown river
two ducks pulling
threads of mist

searchlight at the border
two halves of the
autumn sky

Millennium Bridge –
behind me and before me,
cold fog

submerged village
the only visitor
moonlight

morning wind
the library
of fallen leaves

relieved guard's overall –
cloudlets of moonlight
from the sleeves

depth of autumn
horses bow before
the setting sun

doors creak…
sleepwalking around the house,
moonlight

chilly days
chrysanthemums
touched with extra colours

along a damaged road the shuddering moon

streaming
along the disused road,
a river of mist

a subtler fragrance...
full moon
over the orange grove

screams over the harbour
black-tailed gulls
measuring darkness

pond-apple tree
without any fruit –
withered moon

blossoming goldenrods
the loneliness
of the wind

midnight lake
the silver of
yester moons

floating moon…
but the stars have no home
in sea water

divorce papers
autumn rain washing
the hotel terrace

inside the wishing well,
the moon and a pair of
moon-dogs

windswept garden
the rustling of dead leaves
lingers

through the briars
and the brambles,
the camouflaged moon

deep autumn
the morning's make-up
fading in the rain

limestone haze
over a boreen...
the breathing moonlight

———

Boreen: unpaved rural road in Ireland.

Winter

murmuring surge
mussel shells
slightly open

icy beach
a child treads upon
broken bits of seashells

shop window in Lodz
nothing but
this red winter sun

heavy with snow,
barley bows to landing
snowflakes

ribwort leaf
hoarfrost seizes the side
that faces the wind

first snow
a westie's eyes deeper
in her shaggy hair

mulled wine
white winter sun
melts

reading a history book...
the winter stars
farther up

market at midnight
empty oilcloth bag
gathering snowflakes

after the night's storm,
pine needles
dripping with dawn

frosty evening –
inside the church, stillness
and melting wax

a robin hiding
in the snow-crowned hedge
sunrise

winter drizzle
the green of the hills
melts into seawater

outside the sauna,
magpies and blackbirds
taking a snow bath

in a glass of ice water the moon's eye

long boats
more firewood
towards sunrise

winter rye roots
growing through the layers
of time

puddle touched
by moonbeams
the first to freeze

morning sun
the smell of snow
on a rusty barbed wire

sunlit cliffs
winter confined
to the secluded glen

in the ice house
a fireplace
made of ice

coal
the darkness and the heat
of ancient woods

midwinter thunder
war is never
too far away

cranes call
in the dusk
a life beyond

snow-clad peaks –
geese honking ascends
to greater heights

frozen waterfall
the silence
crumbles

The Season of No Season

Haiku and Senryu

river mist
barges transport coal
in both directions

from sunset till sunrise
red-tinted
mountain pines

sunset in the park
a man plays giant chess
against his shadow

outside the opera-house
a songbird singing
Chi sono? Chi sono?

a teenage couple
their rucksacks
misshapen wings

gloomy day
an actor practices a smile
in the mirror

downpour at Carrowkeel
tourists hide
in megalithic graves

evening mist…
in the mirror, the pallor
of ancient faces

police station
a map of Africa
behind bars

immigrant in Dover –
in the large suitcase,
his previous life

among the seabed pebbles,
this one
shaped like a heart

third cup of tea
rain falling
on top of rain

morning breeze –
inside the dolmen, the sheen
of an English coin

badlands of Almeria
a beggar's
dark cracked hand

an aspen
outside the Deutsche Bank
counting its leaves

unscheduled stop
a scarecrow welcomes us
with open arms

Japanese Gardens
old ladies discussing
who's the oldest

Bloomsday
a beach-bound trickle
of straw hats

editorial: murder
rain coming down
in whispers

funeral morning
red roses and the sound
of squashed cellophane

war museum
two gas masks
staring at each other

hospital
night filled with the sound
of breathing

river stillness
an evening mist enters
the lock chamber

abandoned roller-coaster
a curved path of
the setting sun

sleepless night
Mount Bear tossing and turning
in the fog

father's ship barometer –
the weather
many storms ago

sunlit street
and a shady one –
the busy bridge between

wax museum
fear-giggles
from behind Henry VIII

old men on the bench
each keeps
his own silence

a moment's interlude
the young soldier staring
at his hands

candlelit café –
enter
French perfume

spectacles on the sill –
outside, a kissing
couple

sudden shower –
in an open trailer,
naked mannequins

castle keep
ninety-nine steps
to the rising sun

old goat
climbing into a greater
solitude

river tide change –
a paper boat again
on its way to the sea

Halloween
football dummies
in the morning mist

discarded monuments
the afterlife
of shadows

Haibun

Ufa City

The squeaky train plunges into a fishbowl station. No way forward: the rail is buried in sand. Next to the station, another fishbowl, a market, but there is an outdoor bazaar as well, where smells compete with colours and sounds for your attention. Grilling shashlik sizzles over a live charcoal fire sending droplets of burning oil in all directions. The honey man sucks his golden fingers. These tradesmen sitting on empty plastic boxes, what new kind of Silk Road brought them here?

rice dealers…

white Styrofoam grains

tumble in the wind

Life Size

"Sometimes I wish I were tiny and invisible," a girl says on New Year's Day. She is called Tanya. Another Tanya said a similar thing last night. I ask myself if this name will feature prominently in my life this year.

A couple of hours later some other names assemble, the ones that never fancy being tiny. The wind gathers them together in empty lobbies, and chants them one by one accompanied by the tin whistles of draughts.

In the dark gaps between Frankfurt sky-scrapers, there are no stars. "Can you see two luminous neon keys up aloft, 'Minimise' and 'Restore'?" a beggar woman asks me in German, and this question gets her a few coins. Life seems to have been borrowed from the diminished caliph who forgot the magic word "Mutabor".

city echoes…

the rustle

of old paper

The Museum of the Revolution, Moscow

Old revolutions smell of dust. Behind the red plush curtains, a mahogany table with a gramophone that plays songs of forgotten solidarity, the songs now devoid of rage. Nearby, a sculpture of a worker tearing up a cobblestone street. "Cobblestone, a weapon of the Proletariat." Other weapons of street fighting, or are these torture instruments? Flags, plenty of those. Even more portraits. Models of battleships... When you leave, the machine-gun of the armoured car takes aim at the back of your head.

Turkmen carpet:

an Asian-looking face

of Karl Marx

Bishkek City

was once named after Frunze, the Bolshevik general who was operated on simply because Stalin ordered him to undergo an operation. Frunze, strong as a yak, obligingly died – but was soon reincarnated as the Kyrgyz city where the backsides of buildings contrast with the façades. Unsightly cracks, chips and large chunks of missing stucco duly present themselves to those who study signs of the approaching chaos. In the streets, giant print banners test your eyesight: "The Communist Party is Baldyrma. Lenin is Balbuchok." The ethnic Russians, who for their lives can't read Kyrgyz, compete in suggesting obscene translations.

demolished house –

old photographs

tumble in the wind

The Bridge Incident

Wu Scheng-en, an interculturalist, was kidnapped from a bridge by a bunch of anarchists. He later couldn't recall if that bridge was linking the Old and the New, or the East and the West, or even the East and the East, the latter being most likely. One thing he knew for sure was that in the olden days hostilities in that area escalated into the war between the Japanese and the Chinese that half-heartedly pretended to be Koreans.

Wu Scheng-en was told that the condition of his release was the abolition of borders in the region. Locked away out of sight in a derelict pigpen, he was arming himself with patience and measuring the time to come not by the length of years but rather by the milestones of giving up everything he always regarded as important but in present circumstances had to add to the list of immoderations of happy seasons.

stillness in the air

a vulture's shadow crosses

no man's land

Marlboro Town

"People are excellent advertisements of ideas," a cigarette cowboy lets out a small chuckle mixed with a puff of smoke. "We use them as signboards. Welcome to *Marlboro* town."

The afternoon darkens into evening. The crimson sun droops down in the *West* highlighting the façades of buildings and some country folk hanging low overhead outside saloons and shops. The way they smile is supposed to help the visitors to tell the ones from the others.

There are no visitors around, though. Good old boys are quietly rocking on their lassos and exchanging words, rather melancholically.

"Cig cowboys won't go on forever," a man named *Winston* sweats. "They have all kinds of diseases."

"And too many private jokes, which is also sickness," his pal *Kent* ruminates.

The nearby hills are obscured by smoke. The winds have dropped, and the bushes stand stock-still while a *Camel* crosses the painted poster with the *Montana* desert.

crows gather

in the sycamore tree

blood moon

These Flowing Moments

The drowsy air hummed inside the sea-shells of Gothic churches, so I took her to the cinema where we watched our separate lives, and in the second part our life together. "Some day you'll watch part three," I said. "We will," she responded encouragingly.

At home, my feet got surrounded by a sizeable puddle. "Don't melt tonight, please. I am so tired…" she muttered, half-asleep. "Isn't it great that we found out what causes you to thaw and you've got rid of your heart?"

When she fell into deep slumber, I took my heart out of my breast pocket, slid it back under my corium and lay down on the couch. My half-dissolved hand still managed to scrawl the words "End of part two" on a bibliography card, white as snow.

funeral toll –

winter fog curls

around bare trees

Representing His Species

Odd man out, on his own out there, an ash-coloured koala, with fluffy ears and dark blots on his muzzle that resemble open eyes. The black slots of his eyes, however, are almost always closed.

In his dream, he returns to the lost paradise of his ancestors' secrecy. He grumbles contentedly. Or does he groan? Do other creatures of his kind make the same sound?

His motionless figure is sharply defined against the pale sky. A bitter and cutting northerly wind throws shrunken leaves into his enclosure.

his memory

playing backwards

the slow air of time

A Suspension of Time

Little strip of eternity...

— Robert Lowell

Soon after leaving the station the train pauses on a bridge. The night is devoid of sound. The nearby posts have numbers and yellow markings. A falling star stops, and reinvents itself as a signal light. A brighter light highlights the entrance to a café. Across the street, a huge screen shows through the haze. A "Coca-Cola" ad has been swallowed, an ad for a film disgorged.

after dusk it shines,

the hotel called "The End

of the Millennium"

Printed in Great Britain
by Amazon

22069680R00040